THIS WALKER BOOK BELONGS TO:

_____

_____

_____

_____

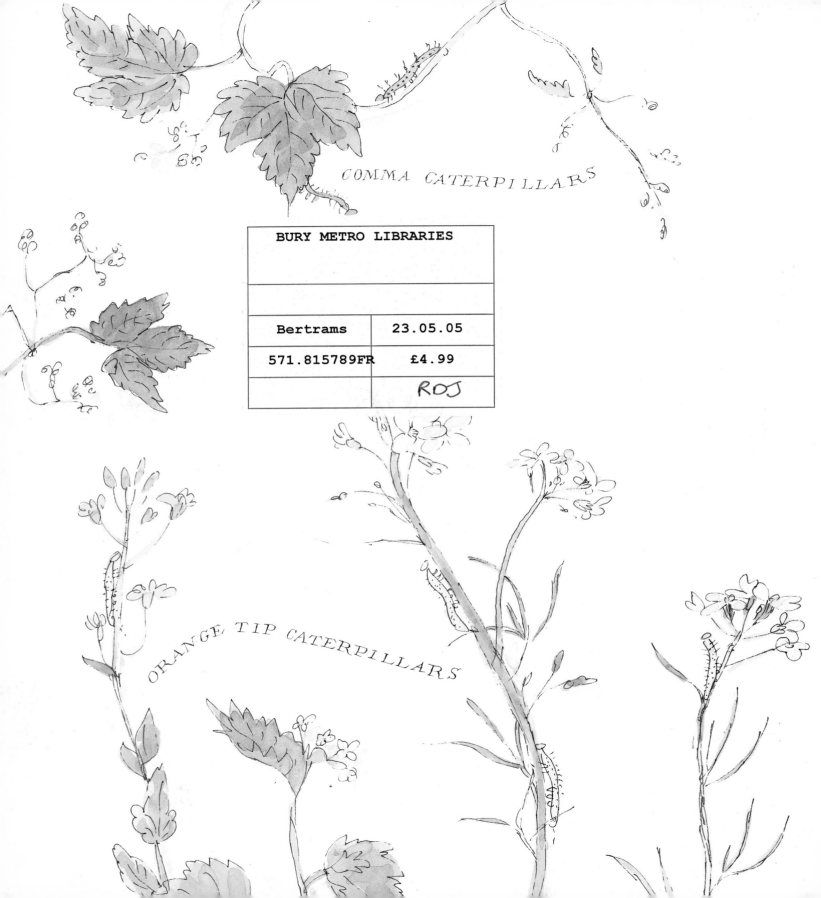

COMMA CATERPILLARS

ORANGE TIP CATERPILLARS

PEACOCK CATERPILLARS

It's impossible to say exactly when
you'll find caterpillars. It depends on where
you live, and what the weather's like, and all sorts
of other things. The eggs I found were laid in May.
They hatched out into caterpillars in June and changed
their skins four times during the next month or so. The first
three times I didn't see it happen, because they changed
inside their tents. But I did see the fourth time…
The caterpillar on the pea sticks pupated
in the middle of July and became
a butterfly in August.

For my grandfather, S.H.K., with love
V.F.
For Robert and Chloe
C.V.

First published 1993 by Walker Books Ltd
87 Vauxhall Walk, London SE11 5HJ

This edition published 2003

2 4 6 8 10 9 7 5 3 1

Text © 1993 Vivian French
Illustrations © 1993 Charlotte Voake

The right of Vivian French and Charlotte Voake to be
identified as author and illustrator respectively of this
work has been asserted by them in accordance with
the Copyright, Designs and Patents Act 1988

This book has been typeset in Calligraphic 810 BT

Printed in China

British Library Cataloguing in Publication Data:
a catalogue record for this book is available from
the British Library

ISBN 0-7445-6282-1

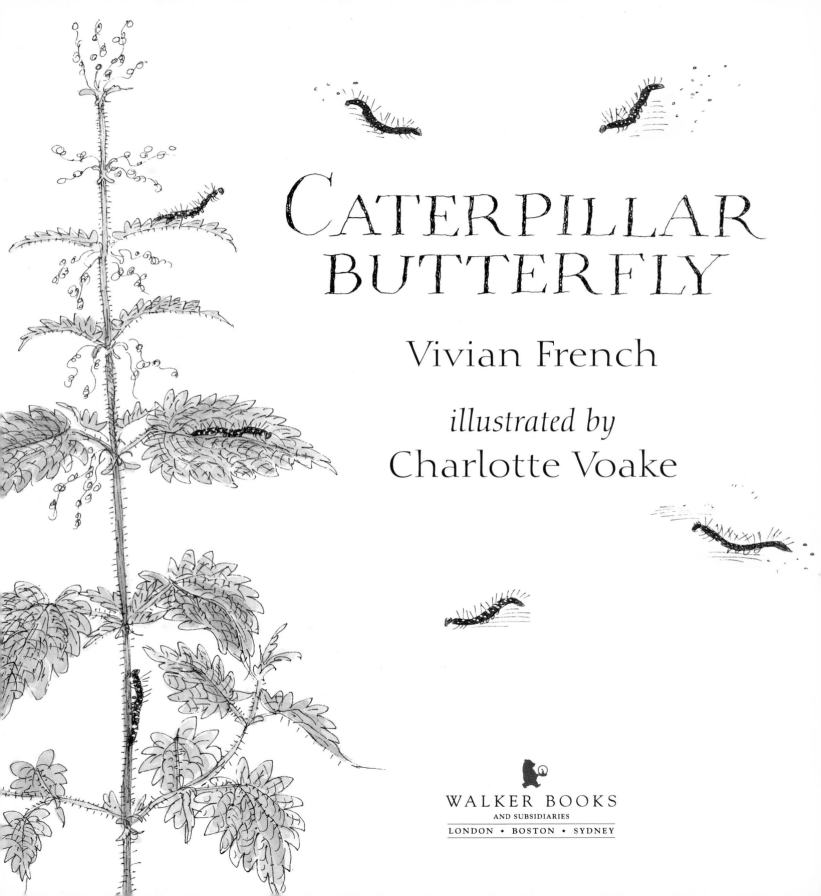

CATERPILLAR BUTTERFLY

Vivian French

illustrated by

Charlotte Voake

WALKER BOOKS
AND SUBSIDIARIES
LONDON • BOSTON • SYDNEY

My father and my grandfather both liked gardening very much, but my grandfather used to grow stinging nettles. My father didn't; he said they were weeds, and rooted them out.

"Why don't you get rid of your nettles?" I asked my grandfather.

"Stinging nettles grow butterflies," he said. "Go and look."

I went and looked. I couldn't see any butterflies, though. My grandfather turned one of the nettle leaves over to show me the bumps on the back of it, but I didn't know what they were.

"Butterfly eggs," said my grandfather.

"What sort of butterflies?"

My grandfather peered closely at the bumps.
"Haven't got my specs on," he said, "but they could
be Tortoiseshells, or Peacocks. They both like nettles.
If you keep an eye on them you'll see when
the caterpillars hatch out."

"Won't they crawl away?" I asked.

My grandfather straightened up
and looked down at me.

"Humph," he said.

"You just keep watching."

So I did.

NETTLES WILL
STING YOU IF YOU
TOUCH THEM,
BUT THEY
WON'T STING
THE CATERPILLARS.

THE EGGS ARE DOME-SHAPED, WITH LITTLE RIDGES. EACH EGG IS ABOUT THE SIZE OF THE TOP OF A PIN.

MOST BUTTERFLIES LAY THEIR EGGS IN ONES AND TWOS, MOVING FROM PLANT TO PLANT. PEACOCK AND TORTOISESHELL BUTTERFLIES LAY LOTS OF EGGS AT ONCE.

Nothing happened at all for
two days. It rained very hard
on the second day, but the
eggs were quite safe.

The next day there were lots and lots
of little tiny caterpillars crawling on the
nettle leaves. The eggs were papery
and empty. I squashed some
with my fingernail.

THE CATERPILLARS EAT
THEIR WAY OUT OF THE
EGGS WHEN THEY'RE
READY TO HATCH,
AND STAY TOGETHER
IN A BIG CROWD.

THEY MAKE A WEB OF
WHITE SILK BETWEEN
THE STEM OF THE PLANT
AND THE LEAVES.
IT'S LIKE A TENT.

WHEN THEY'VE EATEN
ALL THE LEAVES NEARBY,
THEY MOVE ON AND
MAKE A NEW TENT.

My grandfather came over to see

what I was doing.

"Ah," he said, "Peacock caterpillars."

"Do they eat cabbage?" I asked.

I'd seen caterpillars on cabbages.

He shook his head. "Caterpillars are fussy eaters.
If you put a nettle-eating caterpillar on a
cabbage it'll set off to look for
nettles, and if it can't find
any it'll sit down and
die rather than
eat cabbage."

SOME OF THE CATERPILLARS YOU SEE ON CABBAGES ARE

ORANGE TIP CATERPILLARS
EAT LADY'S SMOCK AND
GARLIC MUSTARD.
(SOMETIMES THEY EAT
EACH
OTHER.)

14

COMMA CATERPILLARS LIKE HOPS BEST, BUT SOMETIMES THEY HAVE TO MAKE DO WITH NETTLES.

ABBAGE WHITES. THEY LOVE CABBAGE.

PEACOCK, SMALL TORTOISESHELL AND RED ADMIRAL CATERPILLARS ALL LIKE NETTLES BEST.

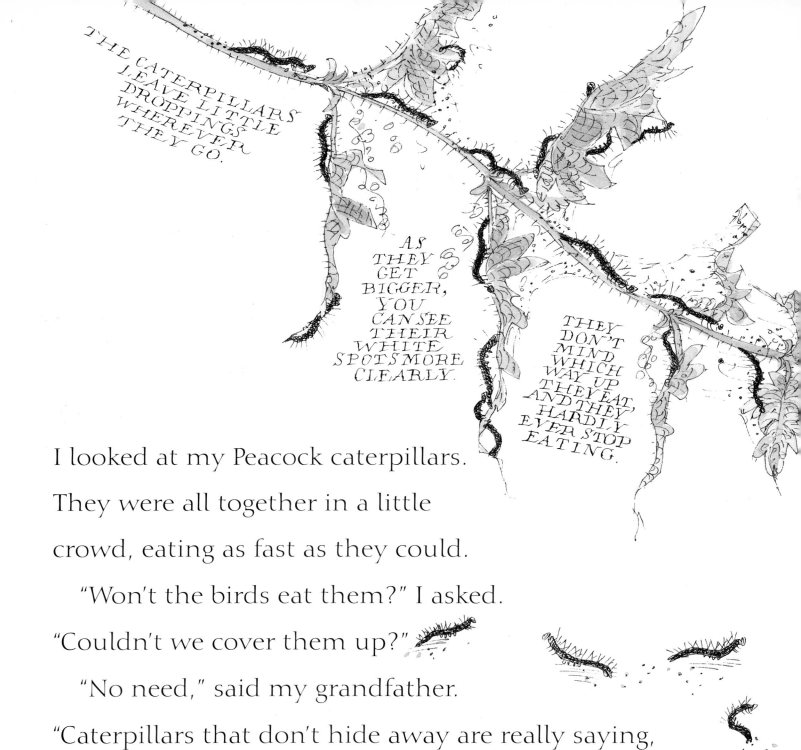

THE CATERPILLARS LEAVE LITTLE DROPPINGS WHEREVER THEY GO.

AS THEY GET BIGGER, YOU CAN SEE THEIR WHITE SPOTS MORE CLEARLY.

THEY DON'T MIND WHICH WAY UP THEY EAT, AND THEY HARDLY EVER STOP EATING.

I looked at my Peacock caterpillars.
They were all together in a little
crowd, eating as fast as they could.

"Won't the birds eat them?" I asked.
"Couldn't we cover them up?"

"No need," said my grandfather.
"Caterpillars that don't hide away are really saying,
'I'm poisonous – keep off!' And the birds know that."

He pulled his pipe out of his pocket and very,
very gently nudged one of the caterpillars.
It curled itself up at once and fell off the leaf.

"There," he said. "Even if something does come along
looking for a snack, the caterpillar might still escape."

"Can I make one curl up?" I stuck my finger out.

"Don't touch them," my grandfather said.

"Some spiny caterpillars can give you a rash,
and other kinds leave a nasty smell on
your fingers. Besides, you might hurt them."

THEY HAVE VELVETY BODIES AND SHINY HEADS.
LOOK AT THEIR SPINY BACKS!
THEY HAVE THREE PAIRS OF LEGS
AT THE FRONT, WITH LITTLE
CLAWS ON THEM, AND
STUMPIER LEGS
FURTHER DOWN.

I went on watching the caterpillars.

They were getting bigger. By the second Saturday in July they had eaten nearly all the plant they had hatched out on and were crawling over the other nettles.

Some of them were lying completely still, though, and not eating at all. All of a sudden one of them gave a little wriggle and its skin split right open. Inside was another brand new caterpillar, and it crawled out of the old skin as if it were crawling out of a sleeping-bag. It looked quite fresh and clean, and it seemed to be bigger than before. All the other caterpillars changed skins too.

WHEN IT'S READY TO CHANGE ITS SKIN, A CATERPILLAR SPINS A LITTLE SILK MAT ON THE LEAF AND FASTENS ITS LAST TWO LEGS TO IT.

I knew something must be eating my caterpillars, because by now there weren't so many of them.

I didn't mind that, but I did mind five days later when I found that every single one of them had disappeared.

"Where have they gone?" I asked. I was close to tears. "Pea sticks," said my grandfather. We marched round the corner of the shed to where the pea sticks were.

"Sometimes one or two come here," my grandfather said.

"Ah, yes, here we are." Sure enough,

there was one of the caterpillars,

hanging head downwards off a pea stick.

And to my amazement, before my very

eyes, its skin began to peel off from

its head upwards ... and shrivelled away.

This time there wasn't another

caterpillar ready to come out.

Instead there was something

like a little soft brown bag, hanging

on the pea stick. It didn't have legs or eyes or

anything, and it dried up into a little case.

My grandfather said that was just what it was,
but the proper name for it was a pupa.

"But where's the caterpillar gone?" I asked.
All the bits of caterpillar were inside the case,
he said, and they were changing.

WHEN THEY'RE READY TO
PUPATE, THE
CATERPILLARS
LEAVE THEIR
NETTLES.

EACH ONE OF THEM
FINDS A
PLACE TO
BE ON ITS
OWN.

IT MIGHT BE UP A
TREE, A FENCE,
A STICK, OR A TWIG.

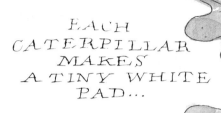

EACH
CATERPILLAR
MAKES
A TINY WHITE
PAD...

THEN
ATTACHES ITS
BACK LEGS TO
IT, AND HANGS
UPSIDE DOWN.

SOON ITS SKIN PEELS
OFF, LEAVING BEHIND
A BEAUTIFUL PUPA.
IT'S GREEN IF IT'S ON
A LEAF, AND BROWN
IF IT'S ON A
TWIG.

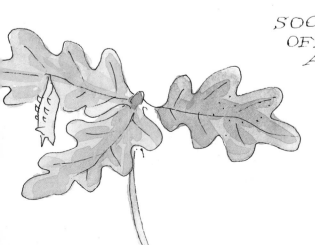

Just this once, I was allowed to bring the stick with the little case on it into the kitchen. I watched for ten whole days and on the tenth day the pupa went very, very dark.

The next morning I was eating my breakfast when my grandfather suddenly said, "LOOK!"

I rushed to see, and the case of the pupa
had split. Something was crawling out ...
but it didn't look a bit like a butterfly.
It was crumpled, and it looked damp,
and it wasn't at all a pretty colour.
    "It must have gone wrong,"
I said, feeling very sad.

Very gently, my grandfather
lifted the stick and put it on
the window-ledge in the sunshine.
The creature crawled slowly up
the stick, and stopped.
Little by little it began to stretch out.
It was just like watching a flower
unfolding itself, only it had
wings instead of petals.

THE WINGS
OF THE
BUTTERFLY
UNFOLD AS LIQUID
IS PUMPED INTO
ITS VEINS.
THE WINGS HAVE
TO DRY FOR AN
HOUR OR TWO
BEFORE IT
CAN FLY.

And the wings began to tremble, and to shine in the sunlight, and then suddenly there it was – a real butterfly, with spidery legs and its wings spread wide open.

It was so lovely that I couldn't say anything at all. Then its wings fluttered and it flew off into the garden – the very newest butterfly there.

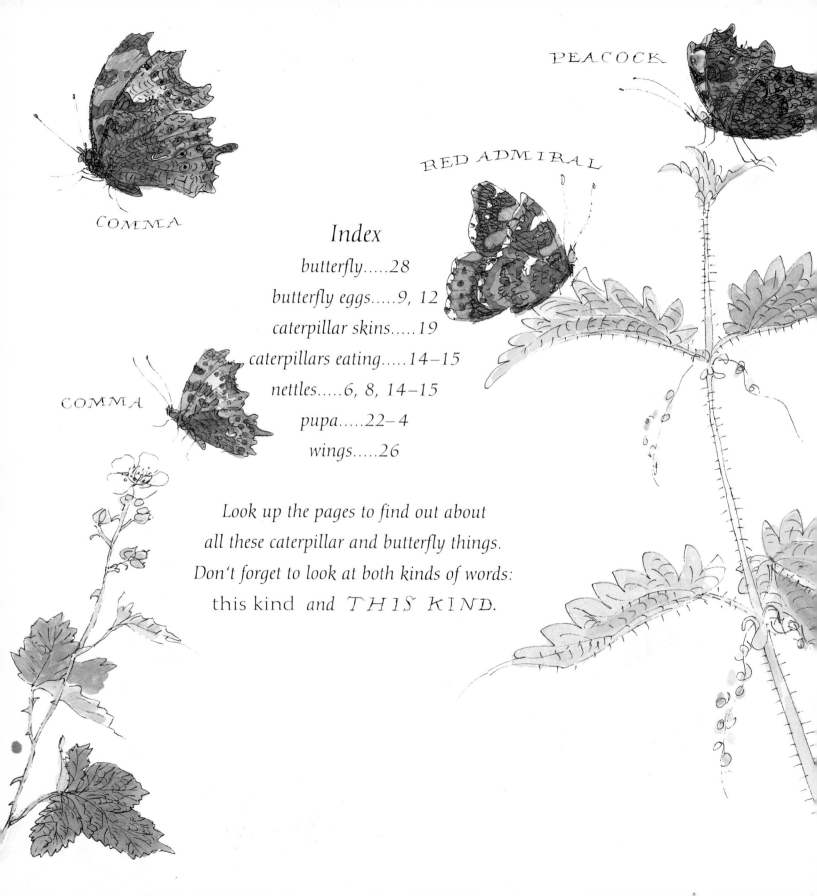

COMMA

PEACOCK

RED ADMIRAL

COMMA

Index

Look up the pages to find out about
all these caterpillar and butterfly things.
Don't forget to look at both kinds of words:
this kind and THIS KIND.

LARGE WHITE

ORANGE TIP

ORANGE TIP

COMMON BLUE

COMMON BLUE
CATERPILLAR

NOTES FOR TEACHERS

The READ AND WONDER series is an innovative and versatile resource for reading, thinking and discovery. Each book invites children to become excited about a topic, see how varied information books can be, and want to find out more.

☞ **Reading aloud** The story form makes these books ideal for reading aloud – in their own right or as part of a cross-curricular topic, to a child or to a whole class. After you've introduced children to the books in this way, they can revisit and enjoy them again and again.

☞ **Shared reading** Big Book editions are available for several titles, so children can read along, discuss the topic, and comment on the different ways information is presented – to wonder together.

☞ **Group and guided reading** Children need to experience a range of reading materials. Information books like these help develop the skills of reading to learn, as part of learning to read. With the support of a reading group, children can become confident, flexible readers.

☞ **Paired reading** It's fun to take turns to read the information in the main text or captions. With a partner, children can explore the pages to satisfy their curiosity and build their understanding.

☞ **Individual reading** These books can be read for interest and pleasure by children at home and in school.

☞ **Research** Once children have been introduced to these books through reading aloud, they can use them for independent or group research, as part of a curricular topic.

☞ **Children's own writing** You can offer these books as strong models for children's own information writing. They can record their observations and findings about a topic, make field notes and sketches, and add extra snippets of information for the reader.

Above all, Read and Wonders are to be enjoyed, and encourage children to develop a lasting curiosity about the world they live in.

Sue Ellis, Centre for Language in Primary Education